Honest to God

Fiona Connolly

BookLeaf Publishing

India | USA | UK

Presentation by *BookLeaf Publishing*

Web: www.bookleafpub.com

E-mail: info@bookleafpub.com

ISBN: 9789357448796

First edition 2021

DEDICATION

To my family, friends and animals, with love

ACKNOWLEDGEMENT

Many thanks to she who suggested the challenge (you know who you are*) to those who have peopled my life and given me food for thought. (*That would be Laura!)

PREFACE

Offered a challenge of writing 21 poems in 21 days, I couldn't resist but take up the gauntlet. What follows are ramblings of varying clarity, but all of which were enjoyable to me (I only made it to 20!). I hope some of them are enjoyable to you too.

The Legend of Tank McNulty

There's a space in that there garden, a very
special space,
It's tortoise shaped, it's EMPTY, where there
used to be a face.
There used to be a face, a shell and four small
feet
But Tank is on manoeuvres now, our hero, so
petite.

They never should have asked these people to
'pet sit',
With attitude so cavalier, they really are unfit.
The Village lights are calling, the world is at his
feet,
We'll never know where he will go, this hero, so
petite.

A look-a-like is needed, the neighbours catch the
bus,
With ready cash, they're shopping at the local
Pets R Us!

A replacement little tortie, the McNulty clan will meet,
They'll never know what happened to the hero so petite.

Kim

'Say Hello to the new girl, she's moved from
over the water',
Despite her frown and bolshie looks, I really felt
I ought to.
I chattered on, without a stop, for two weeks
loud and long.
Eventually I broke her down, despite her being
strong.

A friendship born so long ago, our share of joy
and sorrow
She's in my past, my present too, I know she's in
tomorrow.
My homesick little school pal, who knows me
warts and all,
Here's to you, Kim Kelly, so far we've had a
ball!

Name Games

Do you recall the 90s? We loved a good word
game!
Mum's maiden name and your first pet, would
be your own Porn name.
By far the oldest sibling, the first cat was all
mine,
But my brother and my sister came further down
the line.
We three chose different jobs, so that our
strengths were nicely catered,
One Chloe and two Jolies never did become X
Rated.

Dancing Gill

I always had a yearning to learn to dance – and
WELL!
Chunky framed, no balance, and core strength
shot to hell.
My poor and frazzled teacher tries a million
different ways
To count, direct and navigate me through the
ballroom maze.
Latin dances even trickier, and faster - more's
the pity
My chasse and my lock step never manage to
look pretty.
But on we go, with hopeful hearts, still trying to
advance,
Achieving grace and beauty, moving down the
line of dance.
So Gill, this little ditty, with gratitude is penned,
For each and every lesson, from the start to
bitter end!

Three Hub Caps

My adult life, oft dreamed of in childhood years long gone,
Never did quite follow the schemes I'd settled on.
It seems the world had other plans, and I was unaware,
Single life, and motherhood, and not much cash to spare.
I never thought my dreams would change and hopes be brought so low
A fourth and matching hub cap, and a working radio!

PE

If I could turn the clock back, to school days long ago,
A laminated sick note would be the way to go.
My name was never called out, when teams were put in place,
We all knew (me included) I'd be caught out at first base.
I don't believe my school mates were out to be unkind,
But it really was upsetting, always being left behind.
Sometimes I'd be the Captain, one of this week's 'choosers',
Unsurprisingly I'd gravitate towards my fellow losers.
The PE Teacher (head in hands) would say 'this just won't do,
We need to fill a lesson here, you haven't got a clue.'
My team disbanded, broken up, the losers shared about,
My turn to hit the rounders ball, and guess what
– I'm caught out!

Fairyland

When we were little, siblings three, Daddy
always said,
You know that you're in fairyland when trees
meet overhead.
Down green and narrow country lanes, with
hedgerows either side,
Beneath the leafy canopy, with eyes kept open
wide.
We looked and hoped that one fine day, a fairy
we would see.
My brother claimed a sighting, not my sister and
not me.
The years roll by, we tease him, his fairy
sighting spurned.
But even now, on woodland walks, my head is
upward turned.

The Pussycat and the Owl

One of my closest 'passed over', years before her
time,
It doesn't change a single thing, she's still a
good friend of mine.
She visits in dreams and sends her best, and I'm
thrilled when she pays me a call.
I try to speak, and ask and request, not sure if it
works at all.
On her 2nd anniversary, I knew, I was sure she'd
be there
When I woke the next day, the memory just did
not include HER!
She'd sent me a dream to remember, a dream of
another lost soul,
My Cat, Chilli Pep, who'd gone before, Diane
knew her of old.
Once more I chased a favour, and never again
will I ask,
To prove she could hear, to prove she could see,
just one little tiny task.

Send me an Owl, Di, send me, I know it's a lot
to request,
Please send me an Owl, to prove you're still
there, this'll be the first and last test.

(She did.)

Sharpened Toast

Nan Rev was a fabulous woman, a woman of
courage, so strong,
Moral fibre and backbone abounding, a life that
was full and was long.
By the time she became a Nanna, she excelled at
so much, I could boast,
But her timing and senses had dimmed a tad,
which she proved when she sharpened the toast!

Leopards and Spots

My attitude is flippant, pretty cavalier at best.
I rarely did my homework, never studied for a
test.
A burden which has followed me, and often
made me cry.
It makes for worry and for stress, so WHY –
Fiona – WHY????

We Three

Have you heard of sibling rivalry? We fight, we
learn, we grow.
Have you ever rolled your eyes and wondered
how it is they know?
They know just how to irritate, and how to make
you mad?
There's nothing like a sibling to bring out all
that's bad.
And notwithstanding all I've said, the truest fact
is this,
I wouldn't swap, for all the world, my brother or
my sis.

Mum and Dad

I always knew, without a doubt, my parents
could fix all
From tricky homework questions, to coming
when I call.
No matter when or where, if I and friends
had missed the bus
My Dad would turn up – pronto – and taxi all
of us.
Does every child believe that? Do they think
it in their teens?
I need to tell my only son – I missed out on
those genes!
If you think the world has ended, if you run
out of hard cash
Just tell your Nan and Grandad – they'll be
there in a flash!

Old Bank Clerks

This little rhyming verse or two, will only make some sense,
To those I used to work with, when banking was intense.
Intense in labour, that's to say, with staff in situ many,
We printed cheque books, counted notes and balanced to the penny.
Each working day was started with measures so secure,
We couldn't all turn up at once and enter the front door.
Transactions logged and noted, 'speccy sigs' on file in case
The customer was dodgy, had an unfamiliar face.
Refer Lists for the hapless, those with fluctuating luck,
Who tried to cash a cheque when they were down to their last 'buck'.
How sad, so many bastions re-purposed into bars,
Past glory days forgotten now, their history and ours.

(Speccy sigs = Specimen Signatures)

Gravitate

How is it the like-minded, always seem to find
Another from the Mother Ship who has been left
behind?
It cheers me when I witness such events - and
happily
I, too, was welcomed in like this by Laura, Shaz
and Dee.

The Brownie

She only ever did enough to stay well out of
trouble.
She never went the extra mile, she never left her
bubble.
But on reflection now, as she towards retirement
limps,
Did she just peak to soon when she was Sixer of
the Imps?

The Blazer

The family blazer came to me, it's benchmark
rather high,
From Cousin Jane, who did so well, and through
exams did fly.
I feel she must have taken all the nutrients it had,
For when it came to my exams, my marks were
rather sad.
I felt this rather keenly, and don't wish to be
hard on
Another soul, so now the blazer's buried in the
garden.

Cousin Jane Again

As well you know, I followed after Cousin Jane
in school.
She was the brightest star they had, and I naught
but a fool.
I've asked her since of memories, of what made
her a winner,
She only thought of lessons, I only thought of
dinner.

RE

I'm only really certain, of that which I have seen,
Not sure how much has changed within the
years that lie between.
In RE lessons I sat through, the guilt and fear
was rife
You must be kind and very good, to reach the
afterlife.
Time marches on, and I regret, my focus may
have wandered.
Is it too late to make amends, are all my chances
squandered?
I'll try to smile at strangers, open doors and
kindness show
I'll make the beds, do housework – is this the
way to go?
Maybe just reduce the grumpiness, and less
impatient be.
Did guidelines change, and are school-kids still
frightened by RE?

Of Our Time

Sitting in the car, waiting for the lights to
change,
Distracted, gazing all around, when in my eye
line range,
A school girl crossed the road, but seemed (to
me) not fully dressed,
I couldn't see a knee length skirt, there prob'ly
was no vest.
My mind went back to schooldays, hefty
wenches one and all,
Clothing was obligatory, no running in the hall.
I think she's wearing make up, and expertly
applied,
If she but knew what we looked like, she would
be horrified!
She's of her time, and I of mine, with decades in
between,
Both homeward bound, on foot, in car - Oh
look! – the lights are green.

My Two

My Son is very private and would not want to
be,
Included in a poem, in case someone might see.
But spending time reflecting on all that I hold
dear,
I find I cannot leave a gap, he really should be
here.
To me he is 'the Blond One', his better half is
'Red'
Now 'mentioned in dispatches', I'll put this
verse to bed!